# SIR ISAAC
# NEWTON

*BRILLIANT MATHEMATICIAN AND SCIENTIST*

SPECIAL LIVES IN HISTORY THAT BECOME

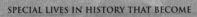

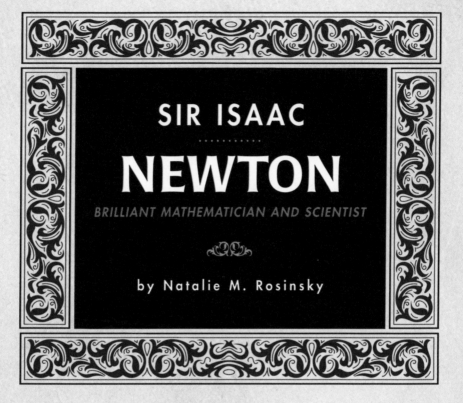

# SIR ISAAC
## NEWTON
*BRILLIANT MATHEMATICIAN AND SCIENTIST*

by Natalie M. Rosinsky

Content Adviser: Margaret Jacob, Ph.D.,
*Professor of History,*
*University of California Los Angeles*

Reading Adviser: Alexa L. Sandmann, Ph.D.,
*Associate Professor of Literacy,*
*Kent State University*

Compass Point Books ✦ Minneapolis, Minnesota

Compass Point Books
3109 West 50th Street, #115
Minneapolis, MN 55410

Visit Compass Point Books on the Internet at *www.compasspointbooks.com*
or e-mail your request to *custserv@compasspointbooks.com*

Managing Editor: Catherine Neitge
Page Production: Bobbie Nuytten
Photo Researcher: Eric Gohl
Cartographer: XNR Productions, Inc.
Library Consultant: Kathleen Baxter

Art Director: Jaime Martens
Creative Director: Keith Griffin
Editorial Director: Nick Healy

**Library of Congress Cataloging-in-Publication Data**
Rosinsky, Natalie M. (Natalie Myra)
  Sir Isaac Newton : brilliant mathematician and scientist / by Natalie M.
Rosinsky.
      p. cm. — (Signature lives)
  Includes bibliographical references and index.
  ISBN-13: 978-0-7565-2209-4 (library binding)
  ISBN-10: 0-7565-2209-9 (library binding)
1. Newton, Isaac, Sir 1642–1727—Juvenile literature. 2. Motion——Juvenile
literature. 3. Physicists—Great Britain—Biography—Juvenile literature.
I. Title.
QC16.N7R64 2008
530.092—dc22 [B]                    2007004595

# SCIENTIFIC REVOLUTION

The Scientific Revolution was a period of radical change in basic beliefs, thoughts, and ideas. Most historians agree that it began in Europe about 1550 with the publication of Nicolaus Copernicus' astronomical theories about Earth and its place in the universe. It ended about 1700 with the landmark work of Isaac Newton and his resulting universal laws. During those 150 years, ideas about astronomy, biology, and physics, and the very way scientists worked, underwent a grand transformation.

Sir Isaac Newton

# Table of Contents

# 1 FAMOUS BUT STILL UNKNOWN

*Chapter*

A friendly bet among well-known figures in late 17th-century London, England, led to a greater understanding of the universe through the most important work of scientific genius Isaac Newton's remarkable life.

In January 1684, astronomer Edmond Halley, architect Christopher Wren, and scientist Robert Hooke attended a meeting of the Royal Society of scientists. Their discussion about what laws might govern the motion of the stars and planets ended in a friendly wager. Wren offered a prize—a book worth 40 shillings—to the first person who could prove these laws mathematically.

Halley (who would have a comet named in his honor) mentioned this bet to his respected acquaintance Isaac Newton the following August. What began

*A dramatic 1729 painting depicts an imaginary monument honoring the memory and genius of Isaac Newton.*

as a playful exchange between friends soon became the most important, serious matter in Newton's life. It was not the prize but the challenge that excited him. He promised to demonstrate why the planets follow an elliptical path around the sun. Newton devoted the next two and a half years to keeping this promise.

Using a new kind of telescope he built himself, Newton began his most influential work. He abandoned his other research projects. He often forgot to eat or sleep. He studied earlier scientists' observations about the stars. Newton used his great mathematical abilities to unite their observations with results from Royal Astronomer John Flamsteed's stargazing as well as his own. He combined this knowledge with information about events on Earth that he studied, such as falling objects and ocean tides. With all this evidence, Newton then mathematically established universal principles about how gravity, force, and motion work and how they are related. These principles became known as Newton's laws.

*A 1702 painting of Isaac Newton hangs in the National Portrait Gallery in London.*

1630) had created controversy when their observations of the stars showed that the planets revolved around the sun. Until their experiments, Western thinkers had upheld the beliefs of ancient Greek philosophers and mathematicians who said that the sun revolved around Earth.

Roman Catholic Church officials continued to maintain this view, which placed people at the center of the known universe, even after Copernicus' and Kepler's observations. The church had even put Italian scientist Galileo Galilei (1564–1642) on trial for heresy for announcing that his own stargazing supported Copernicus' and Kepler's views. Galileo's experiments with falling bodies were another major influence on Newton's far-ranging achievements.

In the years following the publication of the *Principia*, English people began to describe Newton as one of their country's greatest thinkers. His genius inspired many works of art and poetry. English poet Alexander Pope summed up the awestruck public opinion of Newton when he wrote:

*Newton's first law of motion states that an object stays still or keeps moving until a force acts on it. The second law says that a moving object travels in the direction in which that force pushed it. Its speed depends on the strength of the pushing force. In honor of Isaac Newton, modern scientists measure this force in units they call newtons. The third law of motion states that every action has an opposite action of equal strength. Newton's law of gravity says that any two objects in the universe attract each other in relation to their mass and distance from each other.*

*Nature and Nature's Laws lay hid in Night.*
*God said,* Let Newton be! *and All was* Light.

*A romanticized 1827 painting of Isaac Newton pictures him noticing a child's soap bubble and immediately discovering the refraction of light. In reality, it took time for Newton's ideas to develop.*

He became a figure of legend after stories were told and repeated so often about his abilities and discoveries: He had invented the branch of mathematics called calculus. He investigated light and, through experiments, proved its relationship to color. Newton's ability late in life to become a successful government official on top of his other achievements added to his celebrity status.

Today Isaac Newton's achievements continue to influence every field of advanced science. His method of finding scientific principles by gathering evidence and examining it mathematically became and remains the way all skilled scientists work. Newton's research into optics—the science of light and color—led to breakthroughs in lens-making and major developments in medicine and chemistry. His laws about gravity, force, and motion led to significant inventions, such as the steam engine, and are used today in rocketry and computers.

*Isaac Newton (1642–1727)*

Moreover, many everyday technological items in modern society are touched by Newton's genius. As one science historian notes:

> *Everything in the world that is mechanical, that moves around … is described by Newton's laws, and it is those laws which people use to build the everyday things in the world, even things as mundane as washing-machines. The rate at which the*

The genius of
Isaac Newton is
still felt today.

NEWTON
Quii genus humanum ingenio superavit.

spinning bits of the washing-machine
spin round depends on Newton's laws
and you use those laws in calculating the
stresses involved.

Yet underneath Isaac Newton's public image as a genius was a man with real problems and failings—a complicated, sometimes unpleasant person whose interests and desires did not always match his legend. He had some secrets that broke both laws and customs of his time. Some of his first biographers did not know these secrets, while other biographers—worried that revealing them would hurt Newton's reputation—tried to hide the secrets. Our understanding of Newton as both a genius and man has changed over the years. Even today some mysteries remain about what Isaac Newton felt and did. He is world famous but in some ways still unknown.

The stresses, forces, and laws that shaped Isaac Newton began in his unhappy childhood in the English countryside. Some adults did not expect infant Isaac to survive. When he did, many more adults wondered if the young Isaac they saw would ever be capable of managing his own affairs. ❧

*Chapter*

# 2 NO ROOM FOR ISAAC

Isaac Newton was born on December 25, 1642, during a time of enormous strife for Great Britain. A civil war had begun just months before, led by members of Parliament who opposed King Charles I. Parliament and the king had constantly been at odds. Blood had already been shed in battle, with neither side yet emerging as the clear winner. But that Christmas Day, Isaac's mother, Hannah Ayscough Newton, faced more immediate problems than battles miles away from her farm home in Lincolnshire. Her husband, Isaac Newton Senior, had died three months earlier of an illness. And young Isaac was born prematurely. Now she was a widow with a tiny, sickly newborn infant.

When Hannah asked neighbors to fetch a doctor for baby Isaac, they did not hurry. They were sure

*King Charles I ruled England from 1625 until his execution in 1649 at the end of the country's civil war.*

the baby would die long before any help could arrive. Yet their predictions proved wrong; Isaac survived. He spent his first three years in the comfortable, two-story gray limestone house Hannah had inherited from her husband. Even though Isaac Senior—like many people of his time—could barely write his own name, he had been a successful farmer who profitably raised and sold sheep. Hannah had more money and property than many other people living in or near the Lincolnshire village of Woolsthorpe-by-Colsterworth.

Because she was already well-off, it is hard to understand the life-altering decision Hannah Newton

*Isaac Newton was born in Woolsthorpe Manor, which is now a National Trust property and can be visited. Some of Newton's instruments have been placed in the room where he was born.*

made when young Isaac was 3 years old. She agreed to marry a wealthy local minister, Barnabas Smith, and live with him in his home—but the elderly widower demanded that she leave her son behind. As part of her marriage agreement, Hannah asked Smith to sign over a parcel of his own land to Isaac. Perhaps she thought this increase in wealth was worth the separation from her son. From Isaac's view-point, it was not.

Hannah left her toddler at Woolsthorpe Manor in the care of her parents. There the young boy had little contact with his mother for the next seven years—even though he knew she lived just a few miles away. In the distance, he could even see the tall steeple of the North Witham church next door to his mother's new home. Isaac's unhappiness during this period is evident in several ways. Throughout his long life, he never spoke to biographers or wrote about the elderly grandparents who

*Some sources list Isaac Newton's birth year as 1643 rather than 1642. Neither date is really wrong. According to the Julian calendar, Isaac Newton was born on December 25, 1642. Great Britain used this calendar, invented by the Romans, until 1752. That's when Britain switched to the Gregorian calendar, invented in the 1580s and named after Roman Catholic Pope Gregory XIII, who approved it. This new calendar did a better job of matching the date for Easter with the arrival of spring. Many European countries adopted the Gregorian calendar long before Britain did. According to this calendar, Newton was born on January 4, 1643.*

The English Civil War lasted from 1642 to 1649. Members of Parliament and their supporters objected to the actions of King Charles I. They believed he spent money recklessly, wanted to do away with Parliament, and unfairly and illegally favored Roman Catholics over Protestants. The Protestant opponents of Charles I were called Roundheads, because of the plain hats many of them wore. Charles' supporters were called Cavaliers, for the fancier clothing they wore. In 1649, the civil war ended with the defeat of the Cavaliers and the public execution of the king. Oliver Cromwell, a Roundhead leader, became the head of British government.

tended him in his mother's absence. It is as though they made little or no impression on him, or perhaps he wished to forget all about them. The coldness of the elderly Ayscoughs toward their grandson is apparent in the writings the young schoolboy left behind.

Isaac's first formal lessons were taught in small day schools in the nearby villages of Skillington and Stoke. It was common then for students to learn Latin by copying or making up sentences. Using a quill pen and ink made from oak trees, lonely and fearful young Isaac chose to write these sentences (translated from Latin) in his Latin exercise book: "There is no room for me to sit. ... I am sore afraid. ... We desire those things which hurt us most. ... You are sure to be punished." His sadness only increased as he continued to fill the book, and he added these desperate remarks: "No man understands me. ... What will become of me. I will make an end. I cannot but weep. I know not what to do." With some of these words, Isaac seemed to be considering suicide.

In the separate, small notebook Isaac kept for grouping vocabulary words together, the young boy left further evidence of how abandoned he felt. In the section titled "Of Kindred, & Titles," he listed the words *orphan* and *offender*. It is not clear whether the boy believed his mother was the offender or if he thought his own failings and offenses had somehow led to his being left behind—practically an orphan. In either case, Isaac felt great anger as well as pain

*Isaac Newton's childhood home, Woolsthorpe Manor, is just outside Grantham in Lincolnshire.*

when he thought about his mother and stepfather. In later years, he confessed his hatred, writing that one of his "sins" as a young boy was "threatening my father and mother Smith to burn them and the house over them."

In 1653, Barnabas Smith died. Hannah moved back to the Newton manor house in Woolsthorpe-by-Colsterworth, where her parents had been tending Isaac. She sent the Ayscoughs back to their own home. Yet the reunion that Isaac, now almost 11, had longed for brought him pain. He had to share his mother's attention with a half brother and two half sisters he did not know. Six-year-old Mary Smith, 2-year-old Benjamin Smith, and infant Hannah Smith had never gone without a mother's love. Isaac's bitterness toward the other children centered on Benjamin. Isaac's Latin exercise book soon contained a new sentence, the annoyed remark that "I have my brother to entreat." To his vocabulary list, he followed the title "Brother" with the angry and accusing words "Brawler, Babbler ... Beggar ... [and] Benjamite," clearly indicating his low opinion of him.

In 1655, however, Isaac would no longer have to face his supposed rivals. The 12-year-old was now ready—according to his educated uncle, the Reverend William Ayscough—to benefit from more schooling in another town. Isaac would live away from home and return only for holidays and other school breaks.

*J.M.W. Turner, the most famous English Romantic landscape artist, painted the church in Grantham, where Newton attended school.*

(Living away from home for schooling was common then for boys from well-to-do families.) Hannah Newton Smith respected her brother's opinion. The Reverend Ayscough recommended a private school called King's School, also called the Grantham Free School, in the larger town of Grantham. Isaac soon discovered that life in Grantham brought new pleasures but also new problems. ❧

# Chapter
# 3 "A Sober, Silent, Thinking Lad"

At King's School, Isaac Newton continued to study the traditional subjects for educated young men of his time—Latin, Greek, the literature written in these languages, and the Bible. He owned a book of ancient Greek poetry and another book of ancient stories in Latin. He had also inherited his minister stepfather's library of books about Christianity.

Since mathematics was not one of the traditional subjects then, young Isaac never studied math in school. During the next six years, he picked up mathematics on his own—perhaps by reading books that had belonged to a teacher at King's School who had recently died. Isaac's own reading and the people he knew then were more important than the information he so easily memorized in the classroom.

*Isaac Newton was much happier attending school than spending time at his Woolsthorpe home.*

His uncle had arranged for Isaac to live with the local apothecary, William Clark, and his family in the rooms above the apothecary shop. In addition to William and his wife, Catherine, three children from Mrs. Clark's first marriage lived there. Isaac probably shared a room with one or both of the boys, Edward and Arthur Storer. Isaac's unhappiness over again having to share things with other children is clear in his later written account of his faults. He confessed to "stealing cherry cobs [pits] from Edward Storer" and "denying that I did so." Isaac also admitted to behaving in a bad-tempered way about not getting what he wanted, writing that he had shown "Peevishness at Master Clark's for a piece of bread and butter."

Isaac's quarrels with the Storer boys may even have become violent. It is likely that it was Arthur Storer who kicked Isaac in the stomach one day on the way to school. Many years later, Newton described this event to a biographer. He said that he won the fight that followed, pulling the would-be bully by the ears to a nearby wall and rubbing his nose against it. According to the boys' sister, Catherine Storer, who spoke years later to the same biographer, young Isaac did not get on well with many of his classmates at King's School. She described Isaac then as "a sober, silent, thinking lad" who "never was known ... to play with the boys abroad [outside]." She did remember, however, Isaac's gladly making doll furniture for her.

Some elderly inhabitants of Grantham had vivid memories of Isaac's clever use of tools. He built many mechanical models and devices, using and adapting instructions that he found when he was about 13 in a book called *The Mysteries of Nature and Art*. Isaac copied long passages from this book, which helped him as he built kites, sundials, and small working windmills. One of these windmills even had a special

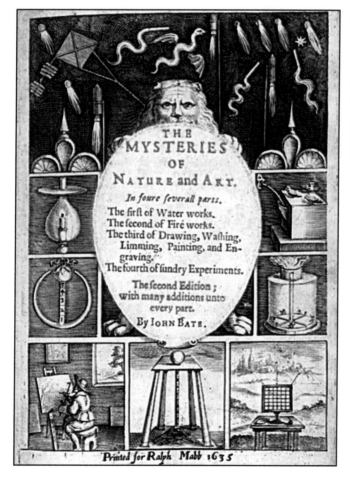

*A popular book by John Bate, written in 1634 and in a second printing the following year, contained directions that Newton used for his projects and experiments.*

wheel built inside it for a mouse. The mouse itself became a power source. When the mouse ran around its wheel, the motion turned a crank that made the windmill's vanes rotate. Isaac also constructed paper lanterns in which he would burn candles to light his way to school on dark winter mornings. Luckily, none of these ever caught fire. His elaborate

*Isaac Newton did not often play with the other students at his elementary school in Grantham.*

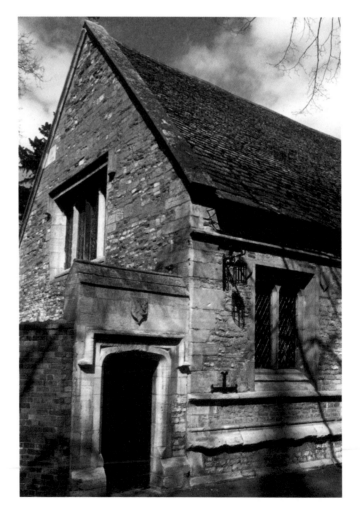

projects included a 4-foot-tall (1.2-meter) wooden water clock that he kept in his attic bedroom.

Catherine Storer was probably correct about Isaac's not often playing with the local boys. His questioning mind and experiments probably set him apart from teenagers who played more ordinary games. Isaac later described what he called his first experiment. On the memorable day of Oliver Cromwell's death in September 1658, a huge storm raged in Lincolnshire. Fifteen-year-old Isaac used this event to measure how strong winds affect how far someone can jump. At first he jumped with the wind, and then he jumped against it. He marked the ground at each point to record and compare the results. This activity probably puzzled or bored some of the other boys. It may even have made enemies of a few of them since—in one version of these events—after the experiment, Isaac unfairly made and won bets about which jump would be longer.

*Military leader Oliver Cromwell took control of Parliament in the 1650s. In 1653, this strong-willed man abolished Parliament and ran the government as the country's lord protector. Cromwell made his Puritan views of moral behavior the law of the land. Each Sunday everyone had to attend church. Attending theater performances, gambling, and getting drunk were forbidden. Punishment for breaking these laws was swift and harsh. When Cromwell died in 1658, his son Richard inherited the government position but lost it. In 1660, Charles II, the son of executed King Charles I, became the new king of England.*

The passage of time may have influenced Catherine Storer's memories of her childhood friendship with Isaac Newton. The renowned scientist's first biographers interviewed her when she was a very old woman. She told them that she and Newton had been sweethearts. She even claimed that they had planned to marry. Perhaps she believed this. Possibly, she just wished history to describe her as being close to the famous man. For many years, this false story about young Newton's boyhood romance was part of biographies written about him.

Catherine did not know about all of Isaac's activities. The quiet boy she remembered was actually busier and happier than she knew—certainly happier than he had been at home in Woolsthorpe. Instead of despairing sentences, his exercise books were now filled with information he found fascinating. Clark's apothecary shop, stocked with colorful ingredients for supposed cures, was a further source of exciting bits of knowledge. Recipes for making chalk, dyes, and even gold ink filled the pages of one of his exercise books. Gold ink, Isaac wrote, could be made by punching a small hole into a fresh egg, adding mercury to its yolk, and sealing the hole with wax for several weeks. Placing the egg back under a hen as it aged was the best way to guarantee the ink would turn out well.

Because paper was expensive, Isaac used tiny handwriting to cram as many as 36 lines of such notes onto each 3-by-5-inch (7.6-by-12.7-centimeter) page of his exercise books. Revealing how little people actually knew then about disease,

Isaac also solemnly included several recipes for medicines that now seem very strange. Many illnesses, he wrote, could be helped by swallowing a "small portion of mint and wormwood and 300 millipedes well beaten (when their heads are pulled off) … [and added to] four gallons of ale." Isaac did not record ever trying out this potion himself. Sometimes, he scribbled on more than notebooks. He would draw pictures of birds, animals, and people on his bedroom walls and even carve his name there and at school.

Isaac continued to easily win praise for earning high grades at school. He began to get along better with Edward Storer. One of Isaac's exercise books from this period indicates that Edward helped him at least once. Its title page declares in Latin, "Isaac Newton owns this book. Edward Storer bound it." Isaac's pleasure in these activities and in his classroom successes was shattered, however, in the fall of 1659, when his mother turned his world upside down. She commanded him to leave school and Grantham and return to the family farm near Woolsthorpe. As a successful sheep farmer, she declared, he would have no use for any further education. ❧

# *Chapter*
# 4 "FIT FOR NOTHING BUT THE UNIVERSITY"

Hannah Newton Smith's plans for her son were not unusual for that time and place. Nearly 17 years old, Isaac Newton was now considered a young man rather than a boy. Since he would inherit land and livestock, it made sense that he take on adult responsibilities. Isaac was already far more educated than most farmers in Lincolnshire. If his uncle, the Reverend William Ayscough, had not urged that Isaac attend school at Grantham, his formal education might have ended years earlier. His mother was being practical and following local customs when she ordered Isaac to leave school and come home. She did not understand how unhappy her decision would make him—or how much trouble it would bring to her entire household.

*Isaac Newton did not enjoy the life of an English farmer and was not good at it.*

The next nine months were a tense, difficult time. Uprooted from familiar routines and pleasures, Isaac was sometimes surly. He even lashed out at other people. In the list of his own failings that he later wrote, Isaac admitted to "Peevishness with my mother. With my sister." He even confessed to "punching my sister" and "striking many." The other people he hit were probably some servants, with whom he had a large argument or "falling out."

Sometimes Isaac simply disobeyed his mother's directions. As he reported, one of his "sins" was "refusing to go to the close [enclosed pasture] at my mothers command." Similarly, on days when his mother sent a trusted servant along with him to sell sheep at the local market, Isaac abandoned this responsibility to his companion. Instead of learning how to get the best prices for livestock, Isaac ran back to his room at William Clark's apothecary shop, where he still kept some books. He spent those days reading. Even when Isaac tried to cooperate, problems arose. He was too interested in books and building complicated devices to pay enough attention to farming chores.

Once, Isaac was so busy reading a book he had brought along to a distant pasture that he did not notice when his horse wandered off. The animal found its own way home long before Isaac arrived back. On another day, Isaac was so interested in what he

*Young Isaac Newton much preferred reading to working on his mother's farm.*

was reading that he forgot to return home for supper. After that incident, the servants could not decide if Isaac's bigger problem was being lazy or stupid. On another occasion, the young man built two model waterwheels on a brook instead of tending the herd of sheep in his charge. They ran off and damaged a neighbor's corn. Isaac was similarly careless with the farm's herd of swine.

His lack of attention caused damage so often that neighbors complained to local officials. Hannah Newton Smith had to pay a fine for her son's carelessness. Records from the local court in Woolsthorpe-by-Colsterworth show that on October 28, 1659, Isaac was charged and fined 3 shillings and 4 pence for "suffering his sheep to break … loose." He was

British money is issued in units called pounds. Until 1971, when the British monetary system changed to decimals, there were also smaller units called shillings and pence, or pennies. There were 12 pence to each shilling and 20 shillings to each pound. During Isaac Newton's time, a pound and its parts were worth a great deal—much more than they are today. A loaf of bread then cost only 1 pence. Servants worked a whole year for just 2 or 3 pounds (worth about $650 today), plus their food and lodging. Someone who had 500 pounds a year was considered rich (worth more than $100,000 today). A fine of 3 shillings (about $30 today) and tuition of 40 shillings were not small amounts of money in the 1600s.

also charged and had to pay separate 1 shilling fines for "suffering his swine to trespass in the corn fields" and for "suffering the fence belonging to his yards to be out of repair."

Perhaps Isaac's mother had a change of heart after seeing how unhappy her son remained after nine months on the family farm. Perhaps she was tired of the household tensions and additional expenses he caused. Whatever her reasons, in the fall of 1660, Hannah Newton Smith permitted Isaac to return to King's School in Grantham. Her brother, the Reverend Ayscough, and the school's headmaster, Henry Stokes, told her that Isaac needed more study there before he could apply to Trinity College in Cambridge. Stokes was so impressed by Isaac's academic abilities that he offered not to charge the usual fee of 40 shillings for tuition. Perhaps this savings was also important to Isaac's mother. It was clear even to her servants that Isaac was not cut out to be a farmer. As one of his first biographers noted, these uneducated but shrewd workers were happy to see Isaac leave, saying that "he was fit for nothing but the [uni]versity."

During his second stay at King's School, Isaac boarded with Stokes rather than the Clarks. After nine months, Stokes declared Isaac ready for Trinity College. In June 1661, the young man eagerly traveled the 100 miles (160 kilometers) to Cambridge.

*Isaac Newton spent his entire life in England.*

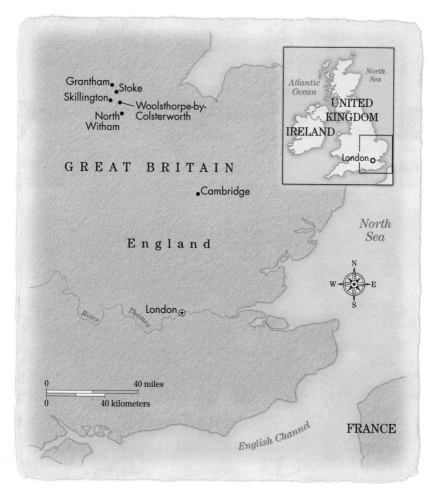

Trinity College is one of 31 colleges that today make up Cambridge University. There were 16 colleges in Isaac Newton's day. This university is one of the oldest in Europe. Scholars first gathered together in the market town of Cambridge, located on the River Cam, in the 13th century. In Great Britain, only Oxford University is older than, and as well known as, Cambridge University. Trinity College itself was founded in 1546 by King Henry VIII.

During his interview with college officials, he had no trouble demonstrating his readiness for university studies. Yet when Isaac actually started college that year, he did so with burdens many other students did not have.

At nearly 19 years of age, Isaac was a year or two older than most new students. This age gap set him apart from his classmates. Something else, however, set him apart even more. Hannah Newton Smith's attitude toward money once again directly affected her son's life. Even though she could easily afford to pay all of Isaac's tuition, she chose not to. Isaac had to pay for part of his college education himself by working as a *subsizar*, or servant, at the college. Subsizars worked for wealthier students or teachers by cleaning their clothing and boots, bringing them meals, carrying wood for their fires, and even emptying the chamber pots used as toilets. For Isaac, used to having servants on the family farm, life as a subsizar must have been particularly hard.

His mother's tight hold on money even extended

to the allowance she gave Isaac. She had a large yearly income of about 700 pounds (about $150,000 today), but records show she gave Isaac only about 10 pounds a year. When he arrived at Cambridge, the young man had enough money to buy a lock for his desk, a quart bottle of ink, a notebook, a pound of candles, and a chamber pot. But after that, he had to budget his expenses carefully. In comparison, other undergraduates often had money to spare. In a bitter twist of fate, Isaac's skill at budgeting set him apart for another reason. He was able to lend small amounts of money to poorer subsizars or gamblers who'd had big losses. These students then resented Isaac for the little money he did have.

Isaac did not make friends during his first, lonely year at Cambridge. But the next years brought dramatic changes to his life. ☙

*Isaac Newton was 18 years old when he began his studies in Cambridge.*

*Chapter*

# 5 "Truth Is My Best Friend"

ଏ∕୧ର୍ଚ

When Isaac Newton arrived in the busy market town of Cambridge in 1661, between 5,000 and 6,000 people lived there. Its narrow, dirty streets often held more people than the young man from Lincolnshire had ever seen at one time. Trinity College, with its hundreds of students, was one of the largest colleges. Its stone buildings, including a chapel and a vast dining hall with a high ceiling, were grander than the churches he had attended.

But even more than that, Newton was shocked by the behavior of people in his new environment. Used to obeying the strict laws of a Puritan government, he was not prepared for the way some students acted under the new, looser laws of King Charles II. Now that drinking and gambling were again legal, these

*The gateway of Trinity College, which Isaac Newton began attending in 1661*

*Even though Newton did not approve, going to taverns was common in the 17th century.*

college students frequently went to taverns. Often they also spent time there with young women, even though college rules still forbade these activities. Newton sometimes played checkers in the college dining hall, but he would not gamble, drink, or flirt with women in taverns. His stricter morals set him apart from many other students and were one reason he did not make friends.

Newton may have been tempted, though. Wrestling with his desires may have led to the outbreak of religious guilt he had in the summer of 1662. That is when Newton wrote down the 49 sins he remembered committing from the time he was a boy up until then. He also resolved to keep a record of any new sins he might commit. In the next months, Newton added nine more sins to his list before he abandoned the project. Perhaps thinking of other students he knew then and their improper behavior, he admitted to "having unclean thoughts words and actions and dreams." Addressing God, Newton further confessed to "setting my heart on money learning pleasure more than Thee." To prevent anyone else from reading his confessions, he wrote this list in a secret code that abbreviated words.

Newton was glad when, during his second year at Cambridge, he met another student who felt and believed as he did. John Wickins entered Trinity College in January 1663. According to an account Wickins' adult son gave many years later, Wickins and Newton met while walking on the college garden paths. Both young men were outdoors that day to escape roommates that they found to be "[d]isagreeable … disorderly companions." Newton seemed particularly "solitary and dejected" to

*After Charles II was restored to the throne, many changes took place in English life. Sometimes called the Merry Monarch, this fun-loving ruler made horse racing and the theater popular as well as legal. Many successful comedies were written during Charles II's reign from 1660 to 1685. This period in English history is known as the Restoration. During this time, Charles was a strong supporter of science as well as of theater, art, and music.*

**45**

The nature of the relationship between Isaac Newton and John Wickins remains one of the mysteries about Newton's life. The two men lived together for 20 years—long past the time they needed to share chambers. Wickins was not a scientist himself, but he worked as Newton's secretary and laboratory assistant. After Wickins left Newton's side to become a minister and marry, the men rarely spoke of each other. They did not meet and wrote each other only a few short business letters. This strange distance and silence after such a long association suggest that the breakup was a painful one.

Wickins. The pair agreed to change roommates and room together "as soon as conveniently they could." What they didn't know then was that they were planning an arrangement that would last more than 20 years. At the time, neither student probably thought any further ahead than the three or four years it took to earn an undergraduate degree.

Trinity College's course of study was typical for that time—a continuation of Greek, Latin, and Bible studies with the addition of more intense study of logic. Yet Newton was much more focused, serious, and intelligent than the typical undergraduate. He already knew some of the required material and quickly learned the rest. But he wasn't ready to just graduate and abandon further study. Newton wanted to branch out beyond the required courses and study topics that interested *him*. A scholarship exam he took and passed in his senior year gave him this chance. Winning the scholarship in April 1664 meant that he would not have to return to Woolsthorpe after graduation. Instead, he was now guaranteed money and living space at Trinity for four more years—time enough to earn the master's degree, or M.A., required to be a college teacher. Newton might then be kept on as a teaching fellow at Trinity.

With his immediate future secured, Newton began to pursue his own scholarly interests, including mathematics. In March 1664, Trinity had appointed its first professor of mathematics, Isaac Barrow. Newton may have attended the lectures that Barrow began to give the following month. By Christmas of that year, Newton had purchased his own copy of René Descartes' work on geometry. Newton read works by other mathematicians, too.

The young man began to puzzle out answers to mathematical problems that not even Barrow could solve. One of these problems involved the time it takes to multiply an enormous series of numbers. Newton figured out a shortcut for this problem—a mathematical rule or formula that is called the binomial theorem. But the intensely religious Newton was not just working on intellectual puzzles. Besides mathematics, he wanted to understand God's will and the meaning of life. He wanted to take on questions that not even the admired Greek philosophers Plato and Aristotle had fully resolved.

Paper remained too expensive to waste. Thrifty

Newton had kept a large, almost blank notebook that once belonged to his hated stepfather. In its pages, the young man now listed 45 topics or questions he wanted to explore in his personal reading and research. These included the mysteries behind such everyday experiences as light, color, and vision. The final topics were ones that are harder to locate in everyday experience—he planned to learn more "of God," "of the Creation," and "of the soul." Perhaps Newton recognized how ambitious his goals were when he scribbled in Latin just above these headings, "Plato is my friend, Aristotle is my friend, but my best friend is Truth."

During the winter of 1664–1665, John Wickins saw Newton behave in the odd ways that became typical for this intense scientist. He ignored food and sleep when focused on a problem. The cat that shared their rooms became fat eating the meals Newton left standing on his supper tray. If the cat did not finish all the food, Newton sometimes ate the cold leftovers for breakfast the next morning. That winter, he missed so many nights of sleep while observing a comet in the sky that, according to an early biographer, he became "much disordered" in appearance and speech.

Newton risked his health in other, even more dangerous ways. Trying to learn more about vision and color, he stared directly at the sun with one eye

*Notes in Newton's personal notebook describe how he conducted eye experiments on himself.*

open until everything he saw appeared red or blue. Newton himself later wrote that "the spirits in my eye were almost decayed" as a result of this experiment. It was days before his sight returned to normal.

Focused on such research, Newton did not pay much attention to his official graduation from Trinity College in January 1665. He and Wickins continued to keep the same odd hours in their shared chambers. Yet events in the summer of 1665 did intrude on their lives and, for a time, significantly change their routines. A tragedy for thousands of people led to the two most remarkable years of Isaac Newton's life. ✥

**49** ✤

# 6  STORIES AND ACHIEVEMENTS

※※※

*I*n the spring of 1665, terror struck the city of London. Citizens began dying of the plague—the painful, seemingly unstoppable disease that had killed millions in Europe during the 1300s. Its symptoms of high fever combined with painful black swellings were obvious. Victims died within days, and doctors did not have a cure. City officials tried to prevent new cases by forbidding large gatherings, but this attempt failed. By the summer of 1665, more than 1,000 people a week were dying in crowded London. The disease spread to other communities.

In Cambridge, university officials acted before disaster could strike there, too. In August 1665, they dismissed all classes and told students and teachers not to return to Cambridge until called back. Isaac

*Isaac Newton used a prism to study light and show that it contained all colors.*

Newton abandoned his scholar's quarters in Trinity College for the safety of his mother's isolated country home. He spent eight months there. University officials called students back in March 1666, but it turned out the officials had acted too quickly. Cases of plague broke out there. By June, Newton had to return again to Woolsthorpe-by-Colsterworth. Nearly another year passed before university officials declared it safe for classes to resume in April 1667.

These plague years were a time of enormous creativity for Newton. He worked during this period on almost all of the mathematical and scientific advances that later brought him fame. Besides the binomial theorem and more mathematics, the scientist had insights into the nature of gravity. He completed further experiments with vision and color and began thinking about how telescopes are made.

Historians and biographers have often labeled this time Newton's *annus mirabilis* or *anni mirabiles*, which in Latin means "miracle year"

*In Isaac Newton's time, people did not know that plague is caused by bacteria carried by the fleas living on rats. About 70,000 people died of plague in rat-filled London. Another 30,000 died in other communities. Their bodies all had the black buboes, or swellings, that give bubonic plague its name. Sometimes this disease is also called the Black Death. In September 1666, a huge fire broke out in London. Blazing for five days, it destroyed more than 13,000 homes and 80 churches. Because so many rats died during this widespread fire, the destruction it caused probably helped to end the plague.*

or "miracle years." Newton himself later wrote that "in the two plague years of 1665–1666 … I was in the prime of my age for invention & minded Mathematics and Philosophy more then at any time since." Yet historians often exaggerated Newton's real achievements during this time, and legends that later grew may have twisted the truth—and may even be lies.

*The Great Fire of London burned for five days and destroyed much of the city, but killed only five people. The plague killed about 100,000 people.*

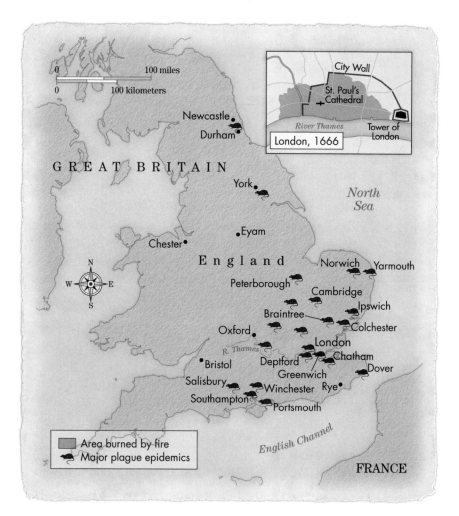

The most famous story about Newton centers on an event that supposedly happened during this stay at Woolsthorpe. According to this legend, Newton was sitting under an apple tree outside the manor house. Seeing an apple fall to the ground, he was inspired to reason through all the principles behind gravity. In the last years of his life, Newton himself helped this legend grow. He told several people about it, including one early biographer who recorded Newton's tale. According to this account:

> *[Newton] thought that the power of gravity, which brought an apple from the tree to the ground, was not limited to a certain distance from Earth, but that this power must extend much farther than was usually thought. Why not as high as the moon said he to himself & if so that must influence her [the moon's] motion & perhaps retain her in her orbit, whereupon he fell a calculating what would be the effect of that.*

Some historians believe that this event happened, but others do not. One biographer maintains that Newton made up the apple story so that his ideas about gravity would clearly date from a time much earlier than those of a later scientific rival, Robert Hooke. Most modern historians who do believe the apple incident occurred also believe that its importance has been twisted out of shape. Newton, they

*Isaac Newton's worktable sits in the garden at Woolsthorpe under an offspring of the famous apple tree.*

say, did not in that instant understand all he later wrote about gravity. Any insight he gained was part of a long, complicated process of thought and investigation. During those months, Newton scribbled some ideas about gravity on the back of an old legal document, but this writing was not necessarily done in a moment's haste.

Newton himself frequently commented that it took time for his ideas to develop. When asked once how he came to understand the workings of gravity, he replied, "By thinking on it continually." Describing his creative process in a letter, Newton similarly explained that "I keep the subject constantly before me and wait 'till the first dawnings open slowly, little by little, into a full and clear light." Newton's remarkable accomplishments, though, are no less great if they did not occur instantly or were not finished during the plague years.

Between 1665 and 1667, Newton completed his earlier work on the binomial theorem. He also developed and wrote papers detailing a new kind of mathematics—calculus, which Newton at the time called his method of fluxions. He conducted further experiments to learn more about vision and color. In one, he again risked his own eyesight. Newton later explained that he placed a small knife "betwixt [between] my eye and the bone as near to the backside of my eye as I could." He then pressed his eye with the flat end of the knife to discover the different colors he might see.

During these years, he also conducted his first experiments with a prism. Newton used this triangle-shaped wedge of glass in a series of tests that revealed that ordinary sunlight—or so-called white light—contains all colors. In his earliest prism

*The Latin word for "flow" or "flowing" is flux. Isaac Newton's mathematical "method of fluxions" helped people to determine the location of a moving or "flowing" item over a period of time. One early practical use of this new branch of mathematics, later called calculus, came in wartime. Military leaders relied on calculus when planning cannon attacks on an enemy. Calculus helped them to figure out where the weapons should be placed so the cannonballs would reach their targets.*

experiment, Newton looked through the glass wedge at different colors. Later he observed how the prism refracted, or bent, the ordinary light shining through it into different colors. Newton's most important and crucial experiment used two prisms. With these, he showed that a color separated out by refraction did not change with further refraction. Red, for example, remained red, and blue remained blue. These experiments also led to Newton's growing interest in telescopes and the lenses they contained.

In April 1667, Newton returned to Trinity College, eager to continue his reading and research. He planned to earn his master's degree, but did not imagine that an even bigger honor would be his. He also did not understand that success and fame would bring new problems into his life. ❧

*Isaac Newton's prism rests on his manuscripts about optics and color at Trinity College.*

*Chapter*

# 7 THE YOUNG PROFESSOR

⌘✕⌘

Isaac Newton and John Wickins had much to celebrate in October 1668. Newton had just earned his master's degree by passing a four-day oral examination. He had also been made a fellow of Trinity College, which meant he would be tutoring undergraduates there. For this work, Newton would receive about 35 pounds (about $8,000 today) in cash each year. He also would get food, lodging, and housekeeping at Trinity, which were worth about another 25 pounds yearly. Newton, however, rented out his newly assigned living space, and he and Wickins continued to share chambers.

During the next year, Newton used his new income to make his living space more comfortable. He hired someone to paint the walls. He bought

*Isaac Newton explained his theories about color to his students at Trinity College.*

a tablecloth and napkins for the dining area and a new rug for his bedroom. He also bought a fancy leather carpet and, with Wickins, purchased a sofa for the living area. After years of making do with a small allowance, Newton took pleasure in ordering and owning two sets of the expensive, special gowns and hats that M.A. graduates wore. Newton also took his first trip to London.

Newton occasionally talked about mathematics with Isaac Barrow, Trinity College's professor of mathematics. Barrow spoke and wrote of Newton's brilliance to others. When Barrow resigned in 1669, Newton was appointed to be his replacement. This was a surprising and wonderful step up in the world. At 27, he was very young to be a professor. Furthermore, this university position, like a few others, was funded by a wealthy man named Henry Lucas. A Lucasian professorship was a special honor that came with a large annual salary of 100 pounds. Newton could now afford to buy a new set of M.A. clothing in red—the

*Isaac Barrow (1630–1677) was a renowned theologian as well as an accomplished mathematician.*

color that indicated a scholar of special importance.

Newton's professorship required that he give weekly lectures. There are no records of how many students attended his first talks, but in later years, an observer reported that even if no students showed up, Newton would "read to the walls." When he had a task to perform, he let nothing stand in the way and thought of little else. He often slept through each day's 7 A.M. worship service in the college chapel because he worked until 2 or 3 every morning. An early biographer wrote that even when Newton had guests over, if "a thought came into his head, he would sit down to paper and forget his friends."

Yet Newton did not have many guests. Apart from Wickins, he made few friends at Trinity, where even the other professors were often in awe of his mind and intense concentration. Other fellows respected Newton's odd ways. According to one early biographer, when new

*Today some researchers believe that Isaac Newton had Asperger's syndrome. This medical condition, which is a high functioning form of autism, affects how the brain works. People with Asperger's are often highly intelligent, but they can be absentminded and sometimes lack social skills. They become caught up with the topics they study, talk mainly about these interests, and often do not communicate well with other people. In addition, they become easily annoyed or angry. This description matches much of Newton's behavior. Other researchers say this description also fits the behavior of some extremely bright people who do not have Asperger's. These investigators do not believe Newton had this condition.*

gravel was placed on Trinity's garden paths, Newton would often use a stick to scratch diagrams and notes into the gravel. The other college fellows were careful to walk around these diagrams for however long they lasted.

During his early years as Trinity's professor of mathematics, some of Newton's lectures to students and writings to other scientists were about math. But most of his lectures and much of his own research emphasized optics. His continued interest in light and color led him to build his own telescopes. The ones he had used before had glass lenses that refracted light. The edges of these lenses acted like a prism, produc-

*Isaac Newton made his own telescope using mirrors instead of lenses.*

ing a halo of colors that interfered with the magnified image. Newton's small but powerful telescopes didn't have this problem. Instead of glass lenses, they used mirrors that reflected light. Newton even built the special tools he needed to make these unusual telescopes, later telling someone that "if I had stayed for other people to make my tools & things for me, I had never made anything of it." These tasks were probably enjoyable ones for someone whose boyhood pleasures included building model windmills.

Fellows of the Royal Society were so impressed by Newton's many accomplishments that in 1672 they invited him to become a member. Newton was thrilled by this honor. Yet membership in the Royal Society brought new problems into his quiet existence. The society's officers persuaded him to write about his theory of colors in articles and letters that would be available to other scientists. When Robert Hooke, another member of the society, learned of Newton's

*The influential Royal Society began informally in the 1640s, when scholars started meeting at Gresham College in London to discuss science. The society became an official organization in 1660, when 12 scholars decided to meet weekly to observe experiments and discuss scientific topics. Britain's King Charles II approved this plan. By 1663, the group was known as the Royal Society of London for Improving Natural Knowledge. It published books and a regular journal containing scientific articles. Membership in the society was an honor. New members, or fellows, were voted in by other fellows.*

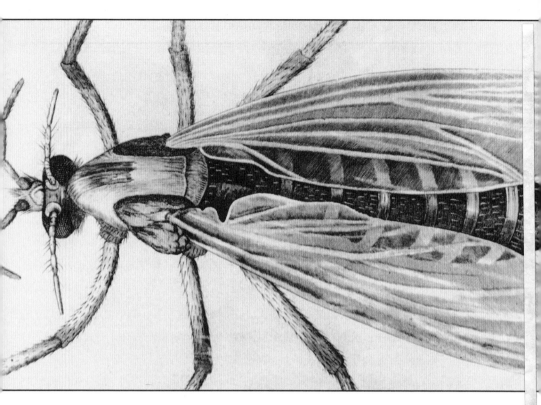

*Robert Hooke described his drawing in* Micrographia *as a "great belly'ed gnat or female gnat."*

ideas, he publicly attacked him. Hooke claimed that the young professor had stolen some ideas from Hooke's own book, titled *Micrographia*, published in 1665. Hooke also said that other parts of Newton's theory about colors were wrong.

Newton was extremely upset by these attacks. He wrote personal and then public letters to Hooke, denying any theft and declaring that Hooke's views were wrong. Other scientists wrote their own opinions about this disagreement. Replying to a French scientist, Newton explained his ideas about how scientists should work. He believed that "the best and safest method of philosophizing seems to be, first to enquire diligently into the properties of things, and to establish those properties by experiments and then to proceed more slowly to hypotheses for the explanation of them." Newton had used this method in researching colors and continued to use it.

Newton found this argument with Hooke so unpleasant that he decided not to publish his optics lectures in a book. He explained this decision in a letter to a Royal Society official, writing that already "I had sacrificed my peace." He continued, though, to correspond with Hooke in private. In one of these letters, Newton described how the work of great scientists such as Descartes had influenced him. In his famous quote, Newton wrote, "If I have seen further it is by standing on the shoulders of giants." Newton simply may have been modest in writing this, but some biographers

Robert Hooke (1635–1703) had many scientific talents. He helped design an air pump, invented a spring-controlled clock, taught mathematics, observed the stars, and examined cells with a microscope. He also illustrated Micrographia, the book he wrote about cells. After the Great Fire of 1666, Hooke helped to rebuild London by surveying it. From 1662 until his death, he set up and conducted scientific demonstrations for each meeting of the Royal Society. Unlike Newton, Hooke liked to gather and talk with people. The two men's scientific feuds may have been made worse by their different personalities.

*Works by Isaac Newton, which grace a lectern at the Trinity College library, can be seen today. The library was designed by Newton's acquaintance Christopher Wren.*

today believe that this remark was also a sly joke at Robert Hooke's expense. Hooke was exceptionally short because of a crippling childhood illness. If Newton was influenced by scholarly "giants," in physical terms Hooke could never have been important to him.

Newton's dislike of criticism only grew stronger in the coming years. As he made new scientific advances and his earlier work on calculus became better known, he drew further comments from other scientists. Whenever these remarks were negative, Newton angrily wrote back. This highly successful man never seemed confident enough to just ignore criticism or admit any mistakes. Today several biographers believe that Newton's unhappy childhood caused his harshness toward critics.

Newton's feuds became well-known to the educated people of his time. All this public attention made life even more dangerous for Newton. This famous man had beliefs and took part in activities that defied tradition and even broke the law. If Newton's secrets had become known then, they could have cost him his job, landed him in prison, or even had him executed. ℰᵥ

*Isaac Newton's unhappy childhood affected him his entire life.*

*Chapter*

# 8 SECRETS AND SORROWS

❧

One of Isaac Newton's dangerous secrets involved religion. His close reading of the Bible had led him to believe that Jesus was not fully divine and ranked lower than God the Father. This idea first surfaced among some Christians in the fourth century, when a priest named Arius began to preach it. It was called the Arian heresy by most Christians, who disagreed with Arius and his followers. Newton was a deeply religious man whose particular kind of Christianity would have cost him his job if it were known.

When Newton became a fellow at Trinity College, he swore—as all new fellows did—to "embrace the true religion of Christ" and either become a priest in the Church of England within seven years or "resign from the college." These Anglican priests, of course,

*Painter Joseph Wright of Derby imagined an alchemist discovering phosphorus during his search for the philosopher's stone.*

did not uphold Arian beliefs. For years, Newton lived with this hard choice before him: keep his position through the sin of a false oath or leave Trinity.

Lucasian professors, however, did not have to become priests. When Newton received this unexpected honor, this huge problem no longer confronted him.

Nevertheless, he still had to keep his unusual view of Christianity a secret. Many respectable people would have been shocked and would have even shunned Newton if they had learned about his religious beliefs. The year Newton became a Lucasian professor, Trinity expelled another fellow for heresy. In his day, people who actively preached Arianism were still arrested and punished as criminals. Even John Wickins may have known little of his roommate's religious views, since the papers he copied for Newton did not include this subject.

Newton also had two areas of research that he kept secret. One was a study of the real dates of events

*Membership in the Church of England—also called the Anglican Church—was required for admission at both Cambridge and Oxford universities. Jews, Muslims, Catholics, members of other Protestant groups, and nonbelievers were all denied a university education. As an alternative to Cambridge and Oxford, the University of London opened in 1826. It accepted students of all religions as well as nonbelievers. Not until later in the 19th century did Cambridge and Oxford admit students of all faiths. That is when women were first permitted to study there, too.*

described and predicted in the Bible. The amount of time and effort that he spent on these matters would have seemed odd to many people. It might have even lowered their opinion of the great scientist. Newton's second research secret, however, was much more dangerous. In many countries, it had landed other researchers in jail and even had them executed.

*Isaac Newton commissioned many portraits of himself during his long life. Only royalty and some noblemen had more.*

Only a few, trusted people knew that Newton was an alchemist—someone who investigated how to combine and transform natural elements. The

so-called science of alchemy had a long tradition. Many alchemists had fantastic, impossible goals. They sought to change cheaper metals into gold, or they sought an elixir, or potion, that would give those who drank it eternal life. This elixir was called the philosopher's stone. Some alchemists believed in and practiced what they called magic. Many alchemists, regardless of their beliefs, had been put in prison and even killed for what others considered to be their evil beliefs and ways.

*Isaac Newton's copy of a diagram of the philosopher's stone*

Newton did not conduct alchemical experiments for wealth or eternal life. He believed that this research, as another alchemist wrote, was a way to

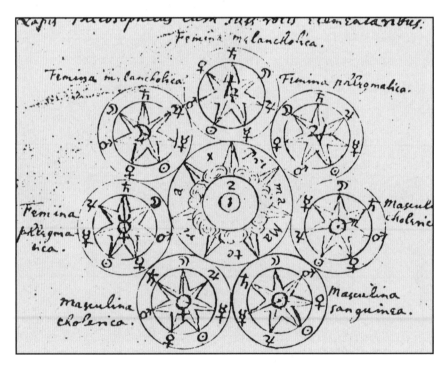

increase "the knowledge of God and secondly the way to find out true medicines." Newton saw alchemy as another way of being a good Christian and a scientist. Later in his life, he defended alchemy to a close relative, saying:

> *They who search after the Philosophers' stone [are] by their own rules obliged to a strict and religious life. That study [is] fruitful of experiments.*

Newton conducted and kept records of many alchemical experiments throughout the 1670s. To avoid discovery, he wrote some of these records in a secret code. In 1673, Newton and Wickins moved into different chambers at Trinity, choosing a courtyard location that gave them more space for these experiments. Newton had a small wooden shed conveniently built right next to their new chambers. Now some of the hot, smelly experiments that involved boiling materials in kettles or melting them in furnaces could be conducted outdoors. Newton built some of these special furnaces himself.

Whenever these experiments required a helper, Wickins was Newton's laboratory assistant. He was one of the few people who knew about Newton's secret research. He even understood that it might have had a physical effect on Newton. By the time Newton was 30, his hair had turned completely gray.

Isaac Newton joked
about his gray hair,
but did he really
suffer from mercury
poisoning? In 1979,
scientists at Cambridge
University tested a
strand of Newton's
hair. It contained many
times the safe level of
mercury for humans.
Mercury poisoning
might have caused
Newton's irritability,
sleeplessness, and
later periods of wild
thoughts. These
behaviors are symptoms
of this disease. They
are also, however,
symptoms of mental
illnesses such as
depression. Newton did
not lose teeth or have
bleeding gums—two
typical and expected
symptoms of mercury
poisoning. Scientists
still disagree about
whether Newton was
poisoned by mercury.

He once half-jokingly told Wickins that it was handling the mercury often used in alchemical experiments that had faded his brown hair so early in life.

Newton was also reluctant to share the results of his more traditional research. He still refused to publish any of it in book form. Only after repeated requests did he send some information about calculus to other Royal Society fellows. They were more outgoing by nature and liked to exchange ideas with other European scientists. One of these was the German mathematician Gottfried Leibniz, who, after receiving the calculus information, mailed his own questions to Newton. When Newton replied in 1676, he gave Leibniz a few bits of information but would not reveal much. Newton excused his secretive nature by writing, "But how to proceed in those [difficult] cases there is now no time to explain."

Keeping ideas and feelings to himself and having few friends made life harder for Newton in 1678 and 1679. He had few ways to relieve the sorrows that those years brought. John Wickins had begun spending less time at their shared home at Trinity. In 1678, he stayed for a total of just six weeks. After that, he made only a few daylong visits to the college. Wickins did not officially leave Trinity until 1684. On the very last day that Wickins visited and then left Trinity, records show that Newton also left. He did not return for a week, although there are no records of where Newton went.

*Newton would often sit at the Woolsthorpe Cemetery to think about his ideas.*

Whatever unhappiness Wickins' leaving caused Newton was made worse when his mother took ill and died in the spring of 1679. Hannah Newton Smith was taking care of her son Benjamin, who was sick, when she caught his terrible fever. Newton journeyed to Woolsthorpe to be with her. According to an early biographer, he took care of her himself, sitting "up whole nights with her" and doing all he could "to lessen the pain." Newton as an adult had not been close with his mother. Yet, during the final three weeks of her life, he may have felt and shown the boyhood love and longing she once inspired.

In the following years, Newton employed two other men to be his assistants. Their accounts of life with the great scientist do not hold any of the mysteries surrounding his relationship with John Wickins. His first assistant, Humphrey Newton (no relation to Isaac), worked for Newton for five years. He left on friendly terms and later named his first son Isaac, in honor of the employer he respected.

Humphrey Newton began copying scientific and Biblical history materials for the scientist in late 1683. This secretary later said that Newton worked constantly. Experiments occupied much time, with the "fire scarcely going out either night or day" in Newton's laboratory furnaces. Humphrey Newton confessed he never understood the purpose of these seemingly important experiments. In 1684, Isaac

*Newton spent many hours in his study at Trinity.*

Newton began a new project. According to his secretary, Newton was so focused on his thoughts that he would "write on his desk standing, without giving himself the leisure to draw a chair to sit down in." This project became Isaac Newton's greatest achievement, the *Principia*. ♒

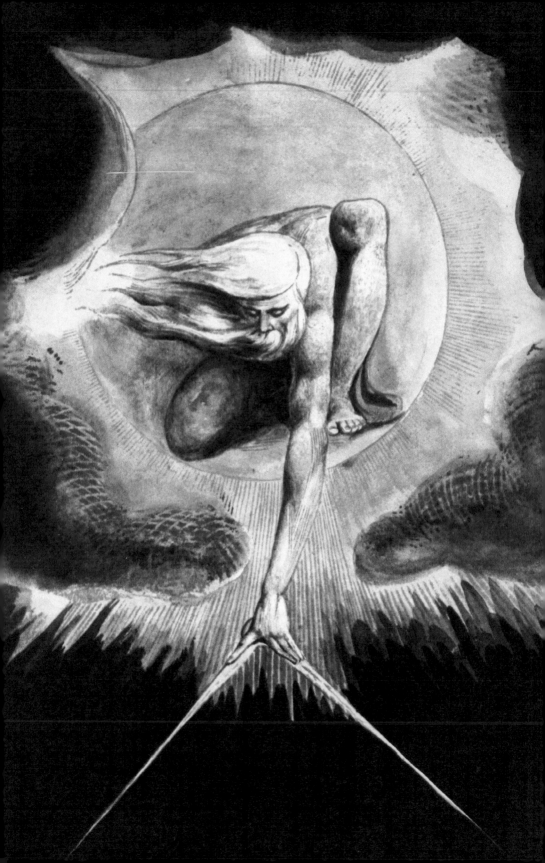

*This most beautiful system of the sun, planets and comets, could only proceed from the counsel and domination of an intelligent and powerful Being. He is eternal ... he governs all things and knows all things that can be done.*

Newton's critics may have misunderstood his views because they did not read the entire *Principia*. His work is filled with complicated mathematics, and it was and remains difficult reading even for scientists. After its publication, one student passing Newton on a Cambridge street supposedly said, "There goes the man that writt [wrote] a book that neither he nor anybody else understands." Nonetheless, Newton's fame for this enormous achievement continued to grow. When King William and Queen Mary took over the English throne in 1689, a special session of Parliament was called. Cambridge University selected brilliant Isaac Newton to represent the school at these important meetings. He spent almost all of 1689 in London, where Parliament met.

*After popular King Charles II died in 1685, his brother James became king of England. Many of his subjects distrusted King James II because he had converted to Catholicism and promoted more rights for Catholics. In 1688, a revolution placed James' daughter, Mary, and her husband, William, on the throne. Mary, who had been raised a Protestant, had married her first cousin William, a Dutch ruler. Both were grandchildren of Charles I. A new Parliament, begun in 1688 and working throughout 1689, supported the rule of William and Mary. Because little blood was shed during the revolution of 1688, it is often called the Glorious Revolution.*

*King William and Queen Mary ruled England jointly until her death from smallpox in 1694. William ruled alone until his death in 1702.*

At that time, Newton began what was possibly the strongest personal relationship of his life. It was with a young Swiss mathematician named Nicholas Fatio de Duillier, who had moved to London two years earlier to advance his career. Fatio was 25 years old and Newton 47 when they met. Their interest in mathematics brought the two men together, but their letters show that their relationship soon became one of deep emotions.

After Newton returned to Cambridge, he learned that Fatio might be seriously ill. He wrote:

*I ... last night received your letter with which how much I was affected I cannot express. Pray procure [get] the advice and assistance of physicians before it be too late and if you want any money I will supply you. ... Your most affectionate and faithful friend to serve you. Is. Newton.*

Another time, Newton wrote Fatio a letter that said, "I intend to be in London the next week & should be very glad to be in the same lodging with you." Records show that Newton spent the following week with Fatio, and later spent another month with him in London. While there is no proof that either man was homosexual, their letters suggest that their affection for one another was romantic.

More than a year later, Newton asked Fatio to move to Cambridge and live with him. But Newton's letter was not detailed enough for the young man. Fatio replied that he would gladly move to Cambridge if only Newton gave reasons for this move that went beyond the younger man's health

*In his lifetime, Isaac Newton was never called a scientist. Scholars who studied nature, the human body, and the stars were called natural philosophers. The word scientist was not used to describe someone involved with these activities until the 1830s. Similarly, the word genius was never used to describe Newton while he was alive. Before his time, this word meant the spark of talent inside every person. In the 18th century, genius began to mean a specially gifted writer or artist. Not until the late 19th century did it also come to describe someone exceptionally gifted in science or mathematics.*

and living expenses. Fatio wrote, "I could wish in that case you would be plain in your next letter." Fatio admitted to Newton, "I could wish sir to live all my life, or the greatest part of it, with you, if it was possible." Newton did not reply in a way that satisfied the younger man. Around this time, Fatio also wrote to his brother in Switzerland, revealing: "My pain comes chiefly from a cause that I cannot explain here … the reasons I should not marry will probably last as long as my life."

Fatio's pain probably came from having feelings and a relationship that tradition and society forbade. In the 17th century, homosexuality was against the law and the morals of most European countries. The forbidden nature of the feelings between Newton and the young mathematician probably contributed to their breakup in 1693. After that, although they did talk about each other, they seldom wrote and met only by accident. Perhaps Newton decided he could not afford another dangerous secret.

The failure of this personal relationship, however, may have harmed the otherwise successful scientist. Deep sadness at separating from Fatio may have contributed to the mental breakdown Newton had in 1693. Many of his symptoms were those of depression. For more than a year, he could not eat, sleep, or concentrate well. He even unreasonably accused people of trying to harm him. Newton later

apologized to his friend, philosopher John Locke, for making such wild remarks and for saying that "twere better if you were dead."

Newton blamed his problems on sleeplessness. A rumor spread that losses from a laboratory fire that year also affected his mind. Today some researchers wonder if mercury poisoning contributed to his breakdown. Whatever its cause, this troubled period marked a turning point in Newton's life. After he recovered, he was ready and eager for a huge change. Alchemists failed to transform lead into gold, but this great scientist would transform himself into a successful government official. ℘

*Newton's dog Diamond may have knocked over a candle that started a laboratory fire and destroyed years of work. This legend about Newton grew in the 19th century.*

## Chapter

# 10 COINING A LEGEND

⧼⧽

Isaac Newton's experience with alchemy was probably helpful when he became warden of the Royal Mint in London in 1696. He already knew much about the careful melting and weighing of metals. These were important in the mint's production of coins. For the next three years, Newton managed a large and difficult project—the recoining of Britain's money. Inside the mint, furnaces roared. Three hundred workmen labored day and night, operating 10 presses that stamped out coins with 50 noisy thuds each minute. Fifty horses also worked in these crowded, smelly quarters, providing power for its mills.

When Newton first moved to London, he lived in a small house alongside the mint, which was then located inside the stone walls of the Tower of

*Isaac Newton was named to the top position at the British mint but never lost his interest in scientific study.*

London. With his ability to concentrate intensely, the constant noise did not bother Newton. His salary of 500 pounds a year (more than $100,000 today), though, permitted the new warden to move into a more comfortable house farther away from his work.

Newton also was responsible for stopping counterfeiters. He could have let hired investigators trap these criminals, but Newton enjoyed being part of these hunts. He went into taverns in the most dangerous parts of London to find, question, and arrest suspected counterfeiters. When convicted, counterfeiters were often put to death. Their fate did not seem to bother Newton, who was responsible for 28 such executions. He even ignored the written plea one convicted man sent him, begging, "no body can save me but you. ... O I hope God will move your heart with mercy and pity to do this thing for me." By this time in his life, however, Newton had hardened his heart to most tender emotions.

What affection he had in him

*In 1695, Britain recalled all coins in use, offering to replace them with newly minted ones. It did this because people in Britain and other countries no longer trusted the value of these used coins. Many had not been made with enough gold or silver. Thieves clipped and stole the edges of some coins, reducing their real value. Other coins were counterfeit. New coins were minted with carefully measured amounts of precious metal. Special machines stamped the coin edges with ridges to make clipping too obvious to succeed. Today 2-pound coins honor Isaac Newton by displaying his words around their ridged edges.*

was directed at his niece Catherine Barton, the daughter of his half sister Hannah. After her father died, 17-year-old Catherine had moved to London to live with Newton in about 1696. Catherine became a clever, attractive woman who remained close to Newton even after her marriage. Her husband, John Conduitt, knew Newton well and became one of his early biographers.

Newton's success at the mint led, in 1699, to his being appointed to its top position—master of the mint. He now had a yearly income of about 2,000 pounds (more than $400,000 today) and felt settled enough by 1701 to resign his professorship at Trinity.

Newton never lost his interest in science, though. When his despised rival Robert Hooke died in 1703, Newton became president of the Royal Society. He did not mind attending each meeting now that Hooke was no longer around. In fact, one of Newton's first official acts was to remove the portrait of Hooke from the society's walls! Newton was not above taking this petty revenge.

His more noble goal for the society was to promote the best scientific research. He declared that worthwhile research "consists in discovering the frame and operations of Nature, and reducing them, as far as may be, to general Rules and Laws,—establishing these rules by observations and experiments, and thence deducing [figuring out] the causes and effects of things." This standard remains in use today.

By 1704, Newton finally felt confident enough to publish *Optics*, the research on light and color he had completed 30 years earlier. In 1705, Queen Anne honored Newton for his scientific achievements by making him a knight of the realm. He was now officially Sir Isaac Newton. The new knight continued to manage affairs at the mint, and with this income

*The Royal Society moved its headquarters to a house on London's Crane Court in 1711.*

he enjoyed life in his fine home. Records show that the fashionable furniture he owned even included two silver chamber pots. Newton took pleasure in having his official portrait frequently painted by well-known artists. He displayed a few of these, but many important people and institutions wanted to display portraits of the great scientist. Newton was preparing the second edition of the *Principia* when, in 1711, his peaceful existence was shattered.

Gottfried Leibniz, the German mathematician Newton had briefly corresponded with in the 1670s, was receiving credit for the invention of calculus. Newton was certain that Leibniz had stolen his ideas. Besides writing to Newton, Leibniz had briefly visited London and spoken to other mathematicians who knew Newton's work. The scientific community took sides in this argument, with many people supporting each man. The debate raged for years. It was at the start of

*Gottfried Leibniz (1646–1716) earned a law degree and studied mathematics on his own. He completed his original work on calculus between 1673 and 1676. He published his first article about it in 1684. Today people agree that Isaac Newton and Leibniz each invented a complete version of calculus independently of each other. Leibniz did not steal Newton's ideas. Newton invented his version first, but the German published his first. During his lifetime, Newton's remarks damaged Leibniz's reputation. Yet Leibniz's easier way of using symbols in calculus, rather than Newton's method, became and remains the calculus system everyone uses.*

this difficult time that Newton, seeking information from John Flamsteed for the second edition of the *Principia*, renewed a feud with this astronomer, too.

Leibniz always maintained that it was possible in scientific advances that "one man makes one contribution, another man another." Newton was not so reasonable. Even after Leibniz's death in 1716, Newton continued to accuse him of wrongdoing and denied the German any credit. In Newton's bitter words, "Second inventors count for nothing." The unhappy boy from Lincolnshire grew in his old age to be, said mathematics professor William Whiston, "the most fearful, cautious, and suspicious" man that he ever knew. The possibility that Leibniz had stolen Newton's work, and the fierce nature of their disagreement, became part of the legends that surrounded Newton.

The great scientist lived a long life in good health, until kidney disease became a problem in the 1720s. Newton remained alert to the end. In his last days, he looked back at his accomplishments and, in what has become a famous remark, described them modestly: "I seem to have been only like a boy playing on the sea shore … finding a smoother pebble or a prettier shell than ordinary, whilst the great ocean of truth lay all undiscovered before me." With his niece nearby, Newton died at the age of 85 on March 20, 1727, in his own bed.

*Isaac Newton's death mask rests in front of his manuscript for the* Principia. *Death masks are casts of a person's face made after death. They were very popular in the 18th century.*

Britain honored its great scientist with burial in Westminster Abbey alongside other important people. Newton's grand monument there displays a larger-than-life figure, surrounded by scientific books, tools such as a telescope and prism, and angels. This

*A marble monument honors Newton at Westminster Abbey in London. His tomb is nearby.*

is the Newton—the public figure seen in many other impressive statues and paintings—that schoolchildren have learned about ever since. And it is this Newton, supposedly inspired by an apple, who has even become part of everyday culture. His name and image appeared in the title of a long-running public television show, *Newton's Apple*, and on stamps issued around the globe. Not until Albert Einstein, whose ideas early in the 20th century expanded Newton's laws, did the world have another celebrity scientist.

Yet the complete picture of the great Sir Isaac Newton is still unfolding. Knowledge of this complicated, often irritable man and his many secrets has grown enormously since the 1930s, when thousands of pages he wrote about alchemy and the Bible were rediscovered. Historians became aware of how early biographers had ignored or hidden many of Newton's secrets, even censoring some letters between him and his friend Fatio. Researchers today continue to examine all of Isaac Newton's writings to learn more about the heart and mind of this scientific genius. ✑

## NEWTON'S LIFE

### 1642

Born December 25 in Woolsthorpe-by-Colsterworth in Lincolnshire, England, during Britain's Civil War (1642–1649)

### 1646

Mother remarries and moves away

### 1653

Mother returns with a half brother and two half sisters to Woolsthorpe

**1645**

### 1646

Blaise Pascal invents the syringe

### 1647

The Society of Friends, or Quakers, is founded in England

### 1653

Oliver Cromwell dissolves the British Parliament and takes the title of lord protector to rule as a dictator

## WORLD EVENTS

**1655**

Begins living with
Clark family in
Grantham

**1659**

Called back to
Woolsthorpe to
learn farming

**1661**

Becomes a student
at Trinity College,
graduating in 1665
and earning a master's
degree in 1668

1655

**1655**

Christiaan Huygens
discovers the rings
of Saturn

**1661**

First modern bank
notes issued in
Stockholm, Sweden

## NEWTON'S LIFE

**1665**

Beginning of the Great Plague in London and Newton's so-called miracle years of work on calculus, optics, and gravity

**1669**

Becomes professor of mathematics at Trinity College

**1672**

Elected as a fellow in the Royal Society and begins feud with Robert Hooke over optics

**1665**

**1667**

John Milton publishes *Paradise Lost*

**1670**

The Hudson's Bay Company is founded

**1673**

Father Jacques Marquette and Louis Joliet explore the Mississippi River and the Great Lakes

## WORLD EVENTS

**1679**

Mother dies

**1684**

Gottfried Leibniz
publishes his work
on calculus

**1687**

The *Principia*
is published

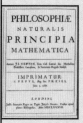

**1685**

**1682**

The French royal
court moves to
Versailles

**1685**

Johann Sebastian
Bach is born in
Germany

## NEWTON'S LIFE

### 1693
Suffers a mental breakdown

### 1696
Moves to London and becomes warden and later master of the Royal Mint

### 1703
Elected president of the Royal Society

## 1700

### 1702
First daily newspaper, *The Daily Courant*, is published in London

### 1696
Denis Papin, a French mathematician and inventor, builds two submarines

### 1703
Peter the Great orders the building of a new Russian capital, to be named St. Petersburg

## WORLD EVENTS

**1704**

Knighted by
Queen Anne

**1711**

Dispute with Leibniz
over invention of
calculus erupts

**1727**

Dies March 20 in
London, England

**1725**

**1714**

Tea is introduced for
the first time into the
American colonies

**1726**

Jonathan Swift
publishes *Gulliver's
Travels*

**1707**

The Act of Union joins
Scotland, England, and
Wales into the United
Kingdom of Great Britain

**DATE OF BIRTH:** December 25, 1642

**BIRTHPLACE:** Woolsthorpe-by-Colsterworth, Lincolnshire, England

**FATHER:** Isaac Newton (1606–1642)

**STEPFATHER:** Barnabas Smith (1582–1653)

**MOTHER:** Hannah Ayscough Newton Smith (?–1679)

**EDUCATION:** Village schools in Skillington and Stoke; King's School (also called the Grantham Free School) in Grantham, 1655–1660, with interruptions; Trinity College in Cambridge, 1661–1668

**SIBLINGS:** Half sister Mary Smith Pilkington (1647–?)
Half brother Benjamin Smith (1651–?)
Half sister Hannah Smith Barton (1652–?)

**DATE OF DEATH:** March 20, 1727

**PLACE OF BURIAL:** Westminster Abbey in London

## FURTHER READING

Anderson, Margaret J. *Isaac Newton: The Greatest Scientist of All Time*. Springfield, N.J.: Enslow, 1996.

Gardner, Robert. *Famous Science Experiments You Can Do*. New York: Franklin Watts, 1990.

Krull, Kathleen. *Isaac Newton*. New York: Viking, 2006.

Parker, Steve. *Isaac Newton and Gravity*. New York: Chelsea House, 1995.

White, Michael. *Isaac Newton: Discovering the Laws of Science*. Woodbridge, Conn.: Blackbirch Press, 1999.

## LOOK FOR MORE SIGNATURE LIVES
### BOOKS ABOUT THIS ERA:

Tycho Brahe: *Pioneer of Astronomy*

Nicolaus Copernicus: *Father of Modern Astronomy*

Galileo: *Astronomer and Physicist*

Robert Hooke: *Natural Philosopher and Scientific Explorer*

Gerardus Mercator: *Father of Modern Mapmaking*

## On the Web

For more information on this topic,
use FactHound.

1. Go to *www.facthound.com*
2. Type in this book ID: 0756522099
3. Click on the *Fetch It* button.

FactHound will find the best
Web sites for you.

## Historic Sites

The Isaac Newton Room
Babson College
231 Forest St.
Babson Park, MA 02457
781/235-1200
Restoration of the parlor of Isaac Newton's
London home and other artifacts of
Newton's life and work, including his
death mask, which form the Grace Babson
Collection of Newtonia

The National Air and Space Museum
The National Mall
Independence Avenue at Fourth Street S.W.
Washington, DC 20560
202/633-1000
The history of flight and space explora-
tion, made possible in part through Isaac
Newton's scientific and mathematical
achievements

**apothecary**
someone who prepares and sells drugs and
medicines; a pharmacist

**brawler**
someone who quarrels, fights, or speaks noisily

**censoring**
removing something considered offensive or
unsuitable from a written work or piece of art

**dejected**
very sad, discouraged, or depressed

**elliptical**
an oval path around something

**entreat**
to ask in a begging way

**heresy**
a belief that goes against major ideas of a religion

**hypotheses**
principles or theories that are assumed to be true
but not yet proven to be correct

**insight**
a clear understanding of the nature or inner
workings of something

**insolent**
disrespectful, insulting, or rude

**kindred**
family relationships or relatives

**scope**
the extent of action or study

## Chapter 1

Page 12, line 3: Richard S. Westfall. *Never at Rest: A Biography of Isaac Newton.* Cambridge, England: Cambridge University Press, 1980, p. 437.

Page 14, line 1: John Butt, Ed. *The Poems of Alexander Pope.* New Haven, Conn.: Yale University Press, 1973, p. 808.

Page 15, line 23: Melvyn Bragg with Ruth Gardiner. *On Giants' Shoulders: Great Scientists and Their Discoveries from Archimedes to DNA.* New York: John Wiley & Sons, 1998, p. 86.

## Chapter 2

Page 22, line 19: Frank E. Manuel. "The Lad from Lincolnshire." *The Annus Mirabilus of Sir Isaac Newton 1666–1996.* Robert Palter, Ed. Cambridge, Mass.: The M.I.T. Press, 1970 (articles originally published in *The Texas Quarterly* 10.3, 1967), pp. 6–7.

Page 22, line 26: Ibid., p.7.

Page 24, line 3: *Never at Rest: A Biography of Isaac Newton*, p. 53.

Page 24, line 18: Ibid., p. 34.

Page 24, line 21: Ibid.

## Chapter 3

Page 28, line 10: Ibid., p. 58.

Page 28, line 13: Ibid.

Page 28, line 25: Ibid., p. 59.

Page 33, line 3: Michael White. *Isaac Newton: The Last Sorcerer.* Reading, Mass.: Addison-Wesley, 1997, p. 23.

Page 33, line 15: Beulah Tannenbaum and Myra Stillman. *Isaac Newton: Pioneer of Space Mathematics.* New York: McGraw-Hill, 1959, p. 37.

## Chapter 4

Page 36, line 5: *Never at Rest: A Biography of Isaac Newton*, p. 65.

Page 36, line 6: Ibid.

Page 36, line 9: Ibid.

Page 36, line 12: Ibid., p. 64.

Page 37, line 15: *Isaac Newton: The Last Sorcerer*, p. 26.

Page 38, line 2: Ibid.

Page 38, sidebar: Lawrence H. Officer. *Purchasing Power of British Pounds from 1264 to 2006.* 10 Jan. 2007. www.measuringworth.com/calculators/ppoweruk/

Page 39, line 3: *Never at Rest: A Biography of Isaac Newton*, p. 65.

## Chapter 5

Page 45, line 7: Frank E. Manuel. *A Portrait of Isaac Newton.* Cambridge, Mass.: Harvard University Press, 1968, p. 63.

Page 45, line 10: Ibid., p. 61.

Page 45, line 27: *Never at Rest: A Biography of Isaac Newton*, p. 74.

Page 45, line 28: Ibid.

Page 46, line 2: Ibid.

Page 48, line 8: Ibid., p. 97.

Page 48, line 12: Ibid., p. 89

Page 48, line 24: Ibid., p. 104.

Page 49, line 2: Isaac Newton. *Questiones quaedam Philosophiae.* The Newton Project: "Bringing the works of Isaac Newton to life." 10 Jan. 2007. www.newtonproject.ic.ac.uk/texts/viewtext. php?id=THEM00092&mode=normalized

## Chapter 6

Page 53, line 2: *Never at Rest: A Biography of Isaac Newton*, p. 143.

Page 54, line 11: Ibid., p. 154.

Page 55, line 11: Ibid., p. 105.

Page 56, line 1: Ibid., p. 174.

Page 56, line 18: Ibid., p. 94.

## Chapter 7

Page 61, line 9: Ibid., p. 209.

Page 61, line 18: Ibid., p. 191.

Page 63, line 8: Ibid., p. 233.

Page 65, line 2: Ibid., p. 242.

Page 65, line 18: Ibid., p. 245.

Page 65, line 24: Ibid., p. 274.

## Chapter 8

Page 69, line 12: Ibid., p. 179.

Page 73, line 1: Ibid., p. 298.

Page 73, line 6: *Isaac Newton: The Last Sorcerer*, p. 121.

Page 74, line 24: *Never at Rest: A Biography of Isaac Newton*, p. 263.

Page 76, line 8: Ibid., p. 339.

Page 76, line 25: Ibid., p. 361.

Page 77, line 3: Ibid., p. 406.

## Chapter 9

Page 79, line 14: Gale E. Christianson. *Isaac Newton and the Scientific Revolution.* New York: Oxford University Press, 1996, p. 83.

Page 80, line 4: *On Giants' Shoulders: Great Scientists and Their Discoveries from Archimedes to DNA*, p. 87.

Page 81, line 1: David Berlinski. *Newton's Gift: How Sir Isaac Newton Unlocked the System of the World.* New York: Simon and Schuster, 2000, p. 172.

Page 81, line 17: *Isaac Newton and the Scientific Revolution*, p. 83.

Page 83, line 1: *Isaac Newton: The Last Sorcerer*, p. 242.

Page 83, line 12: Ibid., p. 238.

Page 84, line 1: Ibid., p. 244.

Page 84, line 3: Ibid.

Page 84, line 7: Ibid.

Page 85, line 2: *Never at Rest: A Biography of Isaac Newton*, p. 534.

## Chapter 10

Page 88, line 22: Ibid., p. 575.

Page 89, line 24: Ibid., p. 632.

Page 92, line 5: Michael White. *Acid Tongues and Tranquil Dreamers: Tales of Bitter Rivalry That Fueled the Advancement of Science and Technology.* New York: Harper Collins, 2001, p. 47.

Page 92, line 10: Ibid., p. 55.

Page 92, line 13: *Never at Rest: A Biography of Isaac Newton*, p. 652.

Page 92, line 23: Ibid., p. 863.

Berlinski, David. *Newton's Gift: How Sir Isaac Newton Unlocked the System of the World*. New York: Simon and Schuster, 2000.

Bragg, Melvyn, with Ruth Gardiner. *On Giants' Shoulders: Great Scientists and Their Discoveries from Archimedes to DNA*. New York: John Wiley & Sons, 1998.

"British Royal Mint—Virtual Tour." British Royal Mint. 29 March 2006. www.royalmint.com/RoyalMint/web/site/Corporate/Corp_museum/touroverview.asp

Christianson, Gale E. *Isaac Newton and the Scientific Revolution*. New York: Oxford University Press, 1996.

Clark, David H., and Stephen P.H. Clark. *Newton's Tyranny: The Suppressed Scientific Discoveries of Stephen Gray and John Flamsteed*. New York: W.H. Freeman and Co., 2001.

Dobbs, B.J.T., and Margaret Jacob. *Newton and the Culture of Newtonianism*. Amherst, N.Y.: Humanity Press, 1995.

"Einstein and Newton 'Had Autism.'" *BBC News*. 30 April 2003. 6 April 2006. http://news.bbc.co.uk/1/hi/health/2988647.stm

Fara, Patricia. *Isaac Newton: The Making of Genius*. New York: Columbia University Press, 2002.

Feingold, Mordechai. *The Newtonian Moment: Isaac Newton and the Making of Modern Culture*. Oxford, England: Oxford University Press, 2004.

Gleick, James. *Isaac Newton*. New York: Pantheon, 2003.

Hall, A. Rupert. *Isaac Newton: Adventurer in Thought*. Oxford, England: Blackwell Publishers, 1992.

Hellman, Hal. *Great Feuds in Science: Ten of the Liveliest Disputes Ever*. New York: John Wiley & Sons, 1998.

Horvitz, Leslie Alan. *Eureka! Scientific Breakthroughs That Changed the World*. New York: John Wiley & Sons, 2002.

Keynes, Milo. "The Personality of Isaac Newton." *Notes and Records of the Royal Society of London* 49.1 (January 1995), pp. 1–56.

Manuel, Frank E. *A Portrait of Isaac Newton*. Cambridge, Mass.: Harvard University Press, 1968.

Newton, Isaac. *Questiones quaedam Philosophiae*. The Newton Project: "Bringing the works of Isaac Newton to life." 10 Jan. 2007. www.newtonproject.ic.ac.uk/texts/viewtext.php?id=THEM00092&mode=normalized

"Newton's Dark Secrets." NOVA. 26 May 2005. 27 March 2006. www.pbs.org/wgbh/nova/newton/buchwald.html

Newton's Tool Box Experiments. 6 April 2006. http://wow.osu.edu/experiments/ntb/ntblist.html

Officer, Lawrence H. *Purchasing Power of British Pounds from 1264 to 2006*. 10 Jan. 2007. www.measuringworth.com/calculators/ppoweruk/

Osler, Margaret J., ed. *Rethinking the Scientific Revolution*. Cambridge, England: Cambridge University Press, 2000.

Palter, Robert, ed. *The Annus Mirabilus of Sir Isaac Newton 1666–1996*. Cambridge, Mass.: The M.I.T. Press, 1970 (The Texas Quarterly 10.3, 1967).

"Sir Isaac Newton." 24 March 2006. www-history.mcs.st-andrews.ac.uk/Biographies/Newton.html

Tannenbaum, Beulah, and Myra Stillman. *Isaac Newton: Pioneer of Space Mathematics*. New York: McGraw-Hill, 1959.

Waller, John. *Leaps in the Dark*. New York: Oxford University Press, 2004.

Westfall, Richard S. *Never at Rest: A Biography of Isaac Newton*. Cambridge, England: Cambridge University Press, 1980.

White, Michael. *Acid Tongues and Tranquil Dreamers: Tales of Bitter Rivalry That Fueled the Advancement of Science and Technology*. New York: HarperCollins, 2001.

White, Michael. *Isaac Newton: The Last Sorcerer*. Reading, Mass.: Addison-Wesley, 1997.

Wills: Arthur Storer, 1686, Calvert County, Md. 8 March 2007. http://ftp.rootsweb.com/pub/usgenweb/md/calvert/wills/storer-a.txt

Natalie M. Rosinsky is the award-winning author of more than 90 publications, including *Light* and *How Scientists Work*. She writes about history, social studies, economics, and popular culture as well as science. Two other Signature Lives biographies by Natalie are *Sarah Winnemucca: Scout, Activist, and Teacher* and *Amy Tan: Author and Storyteller*. Natalie earned graduate degrees from the University of Wisconsin-Madison and has been a high school teacher and college professor as well as a corporate trainer. She lives and writes in Mankato, Minnesota.

## Image Credits